"If you respect the land,

then you will feel the land.

Your experience will be one

that you cannot get

anywhere else in the world."

ABORIGINAL ELDER, JAWOYN PEOPLE
Traditional Owner, Kakadu

A Journey of Discovery

There is something strange about this land, something unexplainable and untouchable, as though we are permitted to walk across it, but can never know its soul. It's a feeling that's always in my heart as I search for the essence of Australia, that elusive quest to capture the secrets of this great land through the lens of my camera. Secrets that I know are there to be discovered, tantalising close at times, like the ghostly arc of a rainbow. Sometimes, in a far corner of the continent where time seems to stand still, that search almost ends. Standing motionless, as if moving a fraction will shatter existence itself, the sheer magnitude of the landscape around me makes my pulse race, numbing my body into a state of expectation. The mood passes, but something happens during those moments of magic. Something very powerful, perhaps an ancient wind passing down the corridors of time brushes by me as I stand in its path.

This is an experience that doesn't happen every day, but often enough to remind me that I am a stranger in this timeless land. Perhaps I sometimes stand in a place where spirits from the dawn of time still exist.

My passion for photography is fulfilled by my search for the spiritual heartland of Australia. I have stood in awe of sculptured landscapes touched by the emerging light of dawn, the fading light of day, and the haunting glow of moonlight. I'm certain that at times the land knows I'm there and I'm greatly affected by that knowledge.

The images in this book reflect my heart and soul dedication to my craft. I have captured the true artistry of nature's work through the simple technique of allowing nature to set the scene. Then I take the picture.

This book is my personal record of this timeless land.

PREVIOUS PAGE
Falls Creek, Snowy Mountains, Victoria.

Late evening light plays among the gnarled shapes of snow gums and the classic lines of Wallaces Hut, a bush shack once used by horsemen of the High Country on their legendary cattle drives.

"Waiting quietly throughout the afternoon for the right light I felt I could almost see and hear the cracking whips and urgent shouts of the drovers thundering by."

The Whitsunday Islands, Queensland.

Morning, on one of the Great Barrier Reef's pure sand cays.

"I added the sunshade to this seascape as a reminder that people are never far away from even the most pristine environment."

OVERLEAF
Hardy's Lagoon, Great Barrier Reef, Queensland.

Midday, and the wondrous magnitude and beauty of this enclosed coral reef system is captured from the air in a grand panorama of form and colour.

"I was concentrating so much on capturing the scene through my camera that I missed the impact of what my eyes were telling me, and it was the photograph itself that finally made me realise the Great Barrier Reef is such a miraculous creation."

Hill Inlet, Whitsunday Island, Queensland.

Day highlights this stunning blend of turquoise water,
white silica sand and green vegetation that complement
the natural arc of Whitehaven Beach.

*"The swirling patterns of this tidal flat and the colours of the
sea make this location a very special place in Australia."*

Wineglass Bay, Freycinet Peninsula, Tasmania.

Dawn breaks, casting pastel light over the incoming tide
and rocky shoreline of this rugged peninsula.

*"I noticed the rock patterns the day before, the beautiful
textures and shapes, and I came back before dawn to
capture the feel and mood of the ocean at first light."*

The Ancient Land

It was born out of the chaos of a planet struggling to find its shape in the whirling maelstrom of an endless universe. Its cradle was a seething landmass of erupting molten rock and cascading fire that created and destroyed mountain ranges over aeons of time as nature prepared to build a new world of colour and light in the darkness of the cosmos. It was the beginning of time for the heartland of Australia.

The landscape of Central Australia has been reshaped by the hand of nature many times in its turbulent 3,000 million year history, as if, through some cosmic design, nature persisted with a grand plan to create, with infinite patience, a place of immense beauty and solitude that would exist for all time.

When the land eventually quietened and the fires of creation retreated deep within the earth, a canvas of immense proportions remained. Great mountains scratched at the sky with jagged fingers of stone - lords of a new world fashioned by the forces of nature. Beneath their shadows stretched desolate plains, plunging canyons of brooding darkness and surreal forests of huge boulders. Vast, shallow seas formed and disappeared with the passage of time. Over millions of years, wind, rain and ice continued to reshape the evolving landscape into the magnificent environment of today.

The heartland of Australia lays beyond mankind's comprehension of time, and every face that it shows reflects the mysterious nature of its distant, violent birth. Its worn-down mountain ranges, its deep gorges carved by long-dead rivers, its sandstone escarpments and the myriad features of endless plains stretching to the horizon are limitless in their variety and spectacular beauty.

Plains of shifting red sands and rolling wind-sculptured dune hills dominate most of Central Australia, often accentuated by fields of spinifex and hardy desert shrubs that flower profusely after rain. Desert dunes rise 30 metres above carpets of rippled flatlands, constantly shifting in the plains wind, living sculptures fashioned by the unseen hands of the gods of nature.

And in tranquil places where time stands still, sandstone bluffs stand as towering sentinels over shaded pools of pristine waters, where desert animals drink and rest in the shade of starkly beautiful ghost gums, and gentle streams flow at the feet of mighty cliffs that glow blood-red in the fading light of day.

PREVIOUS PAGE
Uluru, Northern Territory.

The day's last rays illuminate the heart of Australia.

"While waiting on the spinifex plains I was captivated by the change of mood as clouds banked overhead."

Uluru, Northern Territory.

Morning, and an unusual formation of clouds fan across this great symbol of Australia's interior.

"This place has an amazing sense of strength and power, and that seems to be enhanced by the ray-like pattern of clouds that formed as if from nowhere and disappeared very soon after this photograph was taken."

Uluru, Northern Territory.

Dawn, and the brooding mass of Uluru takes shape as a new day emerges.

"It was completely overcast as daybreak illuminated the sky and the dark line of rock, then pink, flared off the underbelly of clouds before fading suddenly."

Purnululu, (Bungle Bungle) National Park, WA.

Early morning, and this study records the Bungle Bungle
Range's eerie domed towers appearing to defend their open
courtyard against an advancing horde of yellow spinifex.

*"Nothing could say more about the bizarre nature of
Australia's ancient landscapes than this image."*

PREVIOUS PAGE
Tibooburra, New South Wales.

Midday in the harsh outback with stormclouds gathering
intensity and reflecting the red earth of the arid countryside.

*"The windmill blades glinted in the oppressive heat and a sense
of loneliness seemed to hang over the man-made structure as
it stands against the forces of nature."*

Toowoomba, Queensland.

Dusk, and a field of golden sunflowers face east, awaiting
the next day.

"I was overwhelmed by this brilliant sea of colour."

Nabowla, Tasmania.

First light shines across fields of lavender, highlighting vivid columns of colour in the new morning.

"As day broke I was greeted with the splendour and fragrance of lavender blossoms and the company of thousands of buzzing bees."

Cairns, North Queensland.

Sunset, and the night sky provides a moody backdrop as a fierce fire burns through a canefield, clearing rubble from the crop for harvesting next day.

"This is becoming an increasingly rare sight as farmers now harvest their cane green, but the soaring flames against the night have always been a photographer's delight."

Broken Hill, New South Wales.

Late evening on a midsummer's day and clumps of
spinifex cluster on the sunburnt plains like a herd of
strange grazing animals under a threatening sky.

*"I saw this as almost like a landscape from another world
with an army of green-domed spinifex waiting in fear for
the approaching stormclouds."*

OVERLEAF
Montville, Queensland.

Late afternoon and these rolling green pastures typify
the fertile Sunshine Coast hinterland.

*"This is a picture painted on nature's canvas, where
everything fits to make an ideal photograph".*

Beechmont, Queensland.

Afternoon, Gold Coast hinterland, and a lone tree
dominates this peaceful rural setting.

*"The simplicity of this shot is deceptive because there is great
impact and power in the clean lines and vivid colours of just
a tree, fence, sky and meadow."*

High Country, New South Wales.

Towards evening and an old settler's shack prepares for
yet another night in its picturesque rural environment.

*"There is almost a painted feeling to this scene, as if nothing
ever moves and it will remain this way forever."*

Forests & Mountains

Spread across the land are great forests, living reminders of ancient times and the evolution of the Australian continent. Many of these forests are part of mountains, coexisting as they have done since the violent upheavals of nature created the environments that gave them life. Forests and mountains in Australia are as diverse as they are spectacular, stretching from the moody wilderness peaks of Tasmania to the grandeur of the Snowy Mountains, and on to the lush, tropical rainforests of Queensland. Forests and mountains are nature's master strokes in the grand plan of creation. They exist in unity, evolving together for all time.

The wild, untamed beauty of Tasmania's highland interior is the legacy of ice age glaciers that relentlessly carved and convoluted the land into rugged peaks, deep gorges and sheer-sided canyons. It's a formidable landscape that in places is impenetrable and remained largely unexplored until recent years. Primitive temperate rainforests in the west containing rare plantlife and a central plateau dominated by 4,000 lakes are testimony to the wide diversity of terrain in one of the world's last great wilderness areas. In the spectacularly beautiful region of Cradle Mountain and the deep waters of Lake St. Clair, craggy peaks, open moorlands and a profusion of wildlife create a scenic wonderland that symbolises the Tasmanian natural environment.

Victoria's High Country covers an alpine environment at the southern end of the Great Dividing Range, a great mountain chain that stretches north to Queensland along the east coast of Australia. Forests of mountain ash and snow gums bend and twist in bizarre dances shaped by the winds. Purity of air adds a sharp focus to detail and the clarity of a bird's distant call. Vivid colours follow the seasons and in the spring valleys come alive with wildflower blooms. In this unique mountain wilderness of forests, snowfields and panoramic vistas sweeping away to far distant horizons, the immensity of nature unfolds to the human eye.

Northwards in Queensland, lush rainforests cloak mountain ranges in a verdant mantle before tumbling to the sea in a profusion of plant and animal life that has been called the cradle of creation. Here, on majestic peaks overlooking the coastline, and in richly vegetated gullies and waterways along the coast between Townsville and Cooktown, ancient plant species survive in a living nursery of the planet's evolutionary history. These wet tropics nurture families of primitive flowering plants, some found nowhere else on earth, and harbour rare species of animals regarded by scientists as living dinosaurs that could not survive outside their sanctuary. Lowland forests of piccabeen palm stands, thickets of dense undergrowth and jungle vines all compete vigorously for light filtering through the rainforest canopy above. Strangler figs slowly destroy their host trees and become giants of the forest in graphic displays of strength and survival.

PREVIOUS PAGE
Mount Lewis, North Queensland.

Midmorning on an overcast day and time seems to stand
still in this pristine highland rainforest setting.

*"This is one of my first rainforest images and one of my best -
I can still remember breathing the moist, clean air, mixed with
the earthy smells of the living forest around me."*

Fraser Island, Queensland.

Morning sun's rays force through low cloud to highlight
a stand of piccabeen palms in this World Heritage-
listed forest.

*"This very special shot was like a gift, almost a mystical
experience. The sun just broke through for a few seconds
and then it was over, and I just happened to be standing
there to take the picture."*

Numinbah Valley, Springbrook National Park, Queensland.

Day, and the waters of Cave Creek cascade through the Natural Bridge section of the watercourse in a graphic display of nature's artistry.

"Showing the curtain of water cascading into the cave in the most interesting way was a challenge here, and I tried to show it as a contrast to the clearly defined archway leading outside."

PREVIOUS PAGE
Millaa Millaa Falls, Atherton Tableland, Queensland.

Midday and this waterfall creates a perfect
centrepiece in World Heritage rainforest.

*"Time exposure gives the falls a delicate, veil-like
appearance in this pristine forest location."*

The Glasshouse Mountains, Southeast Queensland.

Late afternoon light heightens the rich green fields of this
farm overlooking the plains and mountains beyond.

*"The strange shapes of the distant mountains give this
peaceful rural scene an offbeat edge, as though the
farmhouse doesn't really belong there."*

Atherton Tableland, North Queensland.

Morning mist hovers over dairy farmlands with Mount Bartle Frere, Queensland's highest peak, and Mount Bellenden Ker, in the background.

"This lookout near Millaa Millaa gives a wonderful panoramic vista over this ancient volcanic region."

PREVIOUS PAGE
Dove Lake, Cradle Mountain-Lake St. Clair
National Park, Tasmania.

Early morning, and the old shingle shack on the
shores of the lake strangely fits in perfectly with the
rugged peaks and hardy vegetation that dominate
the Tasmanian highlands.

*"This wonderful combination of natural grandeur and
humble shelter is full of character and the balmy conditions
on the day were ideally suited for this photograph."*

Lake Garrawongera, Fraser Island, Queensland.

Sunrise throws a veil of purple and pink
over an idyllic lake setting.

*"Before sunrise the lake was misty but cleared to create
this reflective image, set off perfectly by the line of
reeds framed in the foreground."*

North West Cape, Western Australia.

Sunset over remote coastland near Exmouth.

*"The last rays of the sun were diffused by cloud, casting
pastel hues over the calm waters of the bay."*

Fraser Island, Queensland.

Twilight casts an eerie glow over the skeleton of the
Maheno, a passenger liner that came to an inglorious end
in 1935 while being towed to Japan for scrap metal.

*"The colours of the sky and movement of the water give
the wreck a mystical effect as night falls."*

Echuca, Victoria.

Early morning on the Murray River and this
famous red-gum wharf, built in the 1880s, bathes
in the soft glow of an emerging day.

*"Autumn colours and water reflections combined
to create a wonderful river setting."*

OVERLEAF
The Twelve Apostles, Great Ocean Road, Victoria.

Sunset lights up these two million year old pillars of stone.

*"The breathtaking colours of this coastline add a haunting
quality to one of Australia's most spectacular landscapes."*

OPPOSITE PAGE
Great Ocean Road, Victoria.

Moonrise, nearing 9pm, and one of Australia's most
stunning rock formations, The Twelve Apostles, takes on
a surrealistic edge as if hovering between reality and
another dimension.

*"This image was completely lit by the moon and gave
me an unusual perspective to work with."*

Fraser Island, Queensland.

Late evening, and a starfish lays dormant under
the pastel hues of a tropical sky.

*"Finding the starfish there in such a wonderful setting
seemed like a gift from an unknown source."*

Peterborough, Victoria.

Day, and the famous London Bridge formation on this windswept southern coastline continues its eternal struggle against the relentless forces of the ocean.

"A few months before I took this shot the land bridge collapsed, reminding me yet again of the awesome power of nature."

OVERLEAF

Mount Kate, Cradle Mountain-Lake St. Clair National Park, Tasmania.

Morning sheds autumn hues over this this heritage-protected cottage built more than half a century ago and still in use by park rangers.

"Made for a photographer's lens, the hut fits this environment perfectly, as if it has always been there, and always will be."

Quamby, Western Queensland.

Late afternoon light paints a blood-red picture
of outback grasslands and hardy gum trees.

*"For me, this rusty truck and Foster's beer sign painted
on the water tank illustrate the carefree mood of
outback Australia."*

Normanton, Northwest Queensland.

New morning light reveals a long-abandoned vehicle,
a symbol of man's presence in the great outback.

*"I found this rusting ute purely by chance and to me it's
a classic illustration of the mood of Australia."*

Einasleigh, North Queensland.

Midday, and the Central Hotel endures the hot summer sun as next door a long-abandoned dance hall leans at a precarious angle.

"This is a classic Australian image with an unusual twist - the old pub refusing to give in as its neighbour, tired and forlorn, surrenders to the demands of time."

Mossman, North Queensland.

Day, and this rusty vehicle gradually succumbs to the relentless growth of tropical vegetation in the grounds of a canecutter's cottage.

"The rusty car and the empty cottage are reminders of a different era, when sugar cane was cut by hand and nobody bothered if machinery was left to the elements once its useful life was over."

Springfield, Tasmania.

Early afternoon and a host of wildflowers transforms
high country bushland into a vibrant garden.

*"It just didn't seem possible that these flowers grew
naturally in such a rugged environment, but there
they were in a brilliant dazzle of colour."*

OVERLEAF
Nandroya Falls, Palmerston National Park, QLD.

Day, and waterfalls cascade through a pristine
World Heritage rainforest setting in Australia's
northern wet tropics.

*"This was shot on an overcast day and has an interesting
composition, with dark shadows leading into light -
a very calming, pure environment."*

Kuranda, North Queensland.

Summer monsoonal rains send floodwaters
thundering over Barron Falls and down to sea.

*"The awesome power of nature in full force is seen here
from Skyrail, a cableway that travels above the rainforest
canopy between Cairns and Kuranda."*

OPPOSITE PAGE
Dorrigo National Park, New South Wales.

A forest stream meanders around moss
and leaf-littered rocks in its midst.

*"Autumn leaves provide a splash of colour
beside a fern struggling to survive."*

Cradle Mountain, Tasmania.

Early morning, and primitive pandanus palms act as eerie
sentinels in the primaeval landscape of the Cradle
Mountain-Lake St. Clair National Park in Tasmania's
rugged highlands.

*"I hiked into this wonderfully surreal country wanting to
photograph a sunrise, but instead mist and drizzle
gave me a shot that is the essence of Tasmania."*

Mossman Gorge, North Queensland.

Morning, deep in the rainforest, and a giant fig tree dominates its surroundings.

"I was impressed by the feeling of strength in this great tree, a true king of the forest."

PREVIOUS PAGE
Undara Dawn, Mount Surprise, North Queensland.

Evening, and sunlight paints a golden glow on an open bushland setting dominated by time-ravaged boulders.

"At this time of the day the Australian bush is magically transformed by the artistic hand of nature."

Devil's Marbles, Northern Territory.

Morning, and these giant spherical boulders, said in Aboriginal mythology to have been laid by the Rainbow Serpent, reflect the colours of their ancient homeland.

"They look less sinister in the daylight, more like sculptured works of art, which is exactly what they are."

Devil's Marbles, Northern Territory.

Evening, and these huge granite boulders south of
Tennant Creek stand balanced as powerful symbols
of the Central Australian landscape.

*"The lone tree silhouetted against the darkening skyline
somehow emphasises the menacing forms of the giant
boulders as night closes in."*

Flinders Chase National Park, Kangaroo Island , SA.

Early morning skies highlight the bizarre profiles of the Remarkable Rocks, a series of strangely shaped granite boulders perched on a curved rockface overlooking Kirkpatrick Point.

"These giant rocks have been hollowed out and shaped by the hands of time, somehow suggesting fierce predators who roamed the earth before the dawn of mankind."

OVERLEAF
Rainbow Valley, Northern Territory.

Late afternoon, and fiery red cliffs near Alice Springs in Central Australia stand guard over the parched surface of a lake waiting for the summer rains.

"I camped there overnight and most of the next day, watching the light and colours change. The feeling of silence was overwhelming and I remember hearing the beat of a bird's wings high overhead."

Kata Tjuta, Northern Territory.

Morning, and a golden glow lights up a spinifex
foreground, highlighting the magnificent rock
formation that evokes the dawn of time.

*"This haunting dreamscape of timeless nature is
one that lives on in my memory."*

OPPOSITE PAGE
Cockburn Range, The Kimberly, Western Australia.

Late afternoon and a wild, crimson sky illuminates
a dramatic bluff high above the surrounding plains.

*"This image portrays the magnificence
of the Kimberly region."*

PREVIOUS PAGE
Rainbow Valley, Northern Territory.

First morning light in the magnificent isolation
of Central Australia.

*"This location is at the end of an arduous drive
but it was worth the effort to experience this truly
beautiful part of our continent. The clarity of
the reflections in the water tell the story."*

Geikie Gorge National Park, The Kimberley, WA.

Late afternoon light reflects the sheer bleached walls
of this magnificent gorge in the placid waters of the
Fitzroy River.

*"This ancient coral reef is a masterpiece of time,
wonderfully crafted by the elements into a showpiece
of nature."*

OVERLEAF
Lawn Hill Gorge, Northwestern Queensland.

Late afternoon view of a lush, freshwater oasis that
has existed unchanged for aeons in the vast arid plains
of outback Queensland.

*"This is a spectacular pocket of greenery teeming with life
out in the middle of nowhere, a place where time has
stood still for countless centuries."*

Dandenong Ranges, Victoria.

Morning, and swirling mist enshrouds this stately
eucalypt forest as it waits for the sun of a new day.

*"The two ferns in front of the vertical lines of these tall
trees make this an interesting composition. In this
photograph I captured the mood of the forest on
a gloomy day."*

OVERLEAF
Dandenong Ranges, Victoria.

Day, and the still waters of the lake reflect a blend of
nature with the boathouse in its midst.

*"I named this image 'romantic boathouse' which I believe
perfectly depicts this peaceful scene."*

Upper Wentworth Falls, Blue Mountains, NSW.

Day, and pristine mountain falls unfold their majesty into the foreground of an image that epitomises the wild beauty of this natural environment.

"All the waterfalls were at their best after weeks of rain and I walked upstream until I found this location, a place which I felt allowed me to achieve my ultimate aim - to work with the perfection of nature."

Mount Lewis, North Queensland.

Midday light enhances the green hues of moss, ferns and tangled undergrowth along a crystal-clear creek meandering through World Heritage rainforest mountains overlooking the North Queensland coast.

"I spend countless hours searching for locations that portray the peace and tranquillity of the rainforest - this is one such place."

OVERLEAF
Lamington National Park, Gold Coast Hinterland, QLD.

Morning light blends with the shadows of giant Antarctic beech trees, 3,000 year-old survivors of the rainforest.

"I was awestruck with the majesty of these trees and the realisation that they had stood here since the dawn of civilisation."

Bell Creek Gorge, The Kimberly, Western Australia.

Morning, and a lone swimmer adds perspective to this spectacular gorge in the remote northwest region of the state.

"This is one of nature's miracles - a cool waterfall and deep pool in one of the most inhospitable places on earth."

Purnululu (Bungle Bungle) National Park, WA.

Sunset, and the Bungle Bungle Range is silhouetted
against a deepening crimson sky.

*"Waiting for the right time to take this picture,
the dome-shaped peaks of this ancient range
took on a mystical quality."*

Mt Isa, Northwestern Queensland.

Late afternoon clouds converge into the
sunset of outback Queensland.

*"The rolling columns of cloud backlit by the sun add
a compelling feature to a landscape that is often
dominated by interesting cloud patterns."*

OVERLEAF
Pentecost River, Western Australia.

Late afternoon river and sky reflect wonderfully in the
Gibb River Road region of The Kimberly, in the remote
northwest of the state.

*"The silence here has a profound effect on the senses,
as if it is a sacred place with many secrets, and
human beings have no right to intrude."*

Hervey Bay, Queensland.

Early morning, and an old timber jetty points across dead
calm water to the horizon and the dawn of a new day.

*"This strong image is composed of clean lines and soft
pastel tones, and there is a sense of expectancy,
as if something strange is about to happen."*

Byron Bay, New South Wales.

Sunrise greets the most easterly point of Australia, bathing the century-old lighthouse in the warm glow of day.

"There are many different angles to photograph this lighthouse, but I like the colours of the eastern sky highlighting the fence, which leads up to the tower itself."

Orpheus Island, Great Barrier Reef, Queensland.

Early morning, and a cloud-covered sun casts its softened light over the ocean-worn boulders and pebbles of this isolated island bay.

"I used a long exposure to capture the milky effect of waves on stone, giving a delicate, smooth look to this tranquil scene."

OVERLEAF
Coffs Harbour, New South Wales.

First light reflects breaking ocean waves on a shoreline of water-worn boulders.

"I call this shot 'Dreamscape' because the time exposure effect gives it a very unusual quality, an ethereal mood that challenges the perceptions of the viewer."

Cape Otway, Victoria.

Early morning and this lighthouse, built by convicts in 1848, continues its lonely vigil over the southern coastline.

"The walkway and the lighthouse, although man-made, seem to somehow fit in with the low, windswept scrub on this remote headland."

OVERLEAF
Welcome Bay, Fitzroy Island, North Queensland.

Morning, and a worn hammock illustrates tropical North Queensland's holiday atmosphere.

"The hammock tied to a pandanus palm, the dinghy on the beach, and the fishing boats out in the bay, remind me of a seafarer's retreat in days gone by."

Lizard Island, North Queensland.

Sunset casts a golden glow across the bay, silhouetting
a timber rowboat on the scalloped sands of a
deserted beach.

*"This photograph is the epitome of pure tropical paradise on
the Great Barrier Reef - I never tire of photographing the
incredible diversity of this wonderful environment."*

Merimbula, New South Wales.

Late afternoon and this water scene evokes the quiet atmosphere of a south coast fishing village.

"This old wooden jetty was just waiting to be photographed at the end of another day in its long life."

Lake McKenzie, Fraser Island, Queensland.

Midday, and a thin veil of cloud breaks up the sky over the stunning tranquillity of an island freshwater lake.

"The colours of this beautiful lake are sensational, like nothing else I've seen anywhere else in the world, and to stand there alone is a captivating experience."

Evans Beach, Cape York Peninsula, North Queensland.

Morning light reveals a sunbleached tree struggling to survive on a remote beach at the northernmost tip of Cape York Peninsula.

"The windswept cloud pattern and the loneliness of the dying tree gives this scene a strange unearthly quality."

Silverton, New South Wales.

Late afternoon, and the Silverton Hotel slumbers in
the fading heat before the evening drinkers arrive.

*"This is a classic outback scene - an old sandstone pub,
isolation, and a dust storm building on the horizon."*

Charleville, Queensland.

Late afternoon sunshine lights up a carriage laden with bales of wool in this outback Queensland train station.

"The glow of harsh summer light seems to be a physical presence here as it softens in the station's shadowed interior."

Longreach, Western Queensland.

Midmorning and a giant windmill dwarfs the Spirit of
the Outback train as it heads across the plains.

*"The windmill and the train are both recognised symbols of the
Australian outback and they came together perfectly for this
shot, which tells the story of the vastness of this land."*

OVERLEAF
Chillagoe, North Queensland.

Early morning and smokestacks stand guard over
long-abandoned smelter ruins.

*"This image has a haunting, metallic quality, a graphic
illustration of nature reclaiming the landscape from
man's interference."*

Boulia, Western Queensland.

Last rays of sunlight cast a glow on this original sandstone
and corrugated iron homestead in outback cattle country.

*"This is a perfect example of how changing light enhances
the character and detail of a structure such as this wonderful
old farmhouse."*

Over Central Australia, Northern Territory.

Afternoon at 36,000 feet, and cloud thunderheads
build up dramatically for an approaching storm.

*"I liked the explosive effect of this cloudbank and took
the shot from the cockpit of an aircraft on the way
to Alice Springs."*

Over the Flinders Ranges, South Australia.

Late afternoon and the sky darkens with the threat
of a violent thunderstorm.

*"There was a definite aura of menace in this cloudscape,
almost as if unseen hands were manipulating the elements
into a destructive force."*

Snowy Mountains, New South Wales.

Morning, and sparkling mountain water cascades in
a veil of spray down a naturally-tiered rockface near
Mount Kosciusko.

*"The shapes and movement of this waterscape paint
a picture of wild natural beauty in the High Country
of Australia."*

Indian Head, Fraser Island, Queensland.

Late afternoon, and the patterned texture and flowing
curves of this wind-formed dune sweep poetically
into a backdrop of blue sea and sky.

*"This image illustrates perfectly how nature manages to
create the most magnificent forms out of the simplest
things - white sand, sculptured by the wind, becomes
a natural work of art, forever changing."*

Simpson Desert, Northern Territory.

Late afternoon light begins to soften the stark
lines of this desert dune.

*"A demanding eight-hour drive rewarded me with
the lonely beauty of this perfect natural creation."*

OVERLEAF
Waddy Point, Fraser Island, Queensland.

Midmorning, on a calm spring day, and this coastline
reflects the beauty of the world's largest sand island.

*"I came across this scene by sheer chance and was
immediately captivated by the crystal clear waves, the cloud
pattern, and the straight line of sand across the bay."*

Holloways Beach, North Queensland.

Daybreak reveals an idyllic tropical setting.

*"This image of a balmy summer morning was captured in
front of my house on the northern beaches of Cairns."*

Mission Beach, North Queensland.

Coconut palms overhang the shores of the Coral Sea.

*"In every person's imagination there is an image
of how paradise should look."*

OVERLEAF
Seventy-Five Mile Beach, Fraser Island, Queensland.

Sunrise and a lonely pandanus palm seems to open
its arms to the emerging day.

*"This composition has a windswept feel to it, with the
primaeval-looking pandanus adding a dawn-of-time quality
to the scene."*

Blue Mountains, New South Wales.

Late afternoon sun paints The Three Sisters formation
blood-red as day begins to fade into night.

*"The sky coloured beautifully for this image, highlighting the
cliff faces above the deep, shadowed valley, and the line of
escarpment ranges far off in the distance."*

Blackdown Tableland, Central Queensland.

A miniature waterfall adds movement to this
rock escarpment.

*"This carved rockface forms a natural amphitheatre around
a fertile garden of palms and ferns."*

OVERLEAF
Manning Gorge, The Kimberley, Western Australia.

Morning in the harsh escarpment country of the
Kimberley region.

*"After an hour's hike into this gorge I was rewarded with
a crystal clear waterfall and calm waters surrounding
a sand Island."*

Rocky Valley Reservoir, Snowy Mountains Victoria.

Sunset near Falls Creek in the High Country.

"Pastel skies approach darkness over rounded granite
boulders and still waters."

Central Coast, New South Wales.

The sun's first rays cast a sepia glow over a deserted beach.

"The rippled-sand effect gives an unusual perspective to this picture."

Hope Vale, North Queensland.

Late afternoon on a silica sand beach traditionally owned by Aboriginal people of the Hope Vale community.

"Tidal sand patterns, a dune ridge, and blue sky reflected in beach pools give this scene an interesting balance."

Huon River, Huonville, Tasmania.

Morning, and reflections of river and boats create a peaceful rural scene suggesting harmony between people and nature.

"Calm water and soft pastels gave a monochrome-type finish to an image that I hadn't envisaged on the morning, yet it turned out to be a fantastic river harbour photograph."

Bicheno, East Coast, Tasmania.

Early morning on the peaceful waters of this
former whaling settlement.

*"Sea and sky seem almost one in this harbour scene, with
the rowboat a necessary part of the local fishing culture."*

Lizard Island, North Queensland.

Morning on the Great Barrier Reef, and across
the sheltered waters of a bay, a sister
island breaks the cloudline.

*"Blue water, a white beach, and a perfect sky tell
the story of life on a tropical island."*

OVERLEAF
Brighton Beach, Victoria.

Noon, and a row of privately-owned bathing sheds adds
a touch of flamboyance to this beach scene.

*"This was a photograph begging to be taken - the sheds
seem out of place on an Australian beach, but defiantly
stand their ground in a mosaic of bright colours."*

PREVIOUS PAGE
Fraser Island, Queensland.

Late afternoon light on Seventy-Five Mile Beach highlights the dramatic effect of a rippled sand blow on the island's shoreline.

"The constantly changing nature of Fraser Island's sand blows have always fascinated me and these knife-edged dunes are accentuated perfectly by scattered cloud and the rippled foreground."

Litchfield National Park, Northern Territory.

Sunset, and termite mounds stand like giant headstones across a timeless landscape.

"As the sun retreated, it was so still and quiet a bird's cry echoed between the mounds."

OVERLEAF
Chambers Pillar, Northern Territory.

Evening, and the eroded peaks of an ancient mountain range dominate the surrounding spinifex and red-earth landscape of Australia's interior.

"This to me typifies the painted desert and worn-down ridges of the oldest continent on Earth. The red-oxide dunes and green spinifex contrast vividly with the deepening blue of the sky."

Roebuck Bay, Western Australia.

Morning, and rock formations near Broome present
an eerie face to the sea and sky.

*"This is a framework of images that nature has carved
from the passage of time."*

Reddell Beach, Broome, Western Australia.

Late afternoon sun turns this rugged beach into a
fiery red landscape.

*"I watched in amazement as the deepening light changed
cliffs, rocks and sand into what I thought an artist's
impression of an alien world would look like."*

Trephina Gorge, Northern Territory.

Early morning and still-water reflections mirror the solitude of this isolated location in Central Australia.

"Sandstone bluffs, ghost gums and crystal-clear water came together perfectly for this wonderful landscape."

Winton, Western Queensland.

Sunset as a mob of sheep is mustered for the night in a confusion of shouts and dust by weary men at the end of another long day.

"The last rays of sun shining through the trees cast a reddish glow on the scene that lasted just long enough to capture this image."

Biloela, Central Queensland.

Midday light illuminates this authentic slab hut to reflect
the lifestyle and hardships of Australia's pioneer settlers.

*"Natural light captured the detail of a bygone era, when
many essentials, including cabins such as this, were
constructed by hand using materials found locally."*

OVERLEAF
Winton, Western Queensland.

Just before nightfall, the violet hues of a fading western
light soften the harsh glare of a summer sun on an
abandoned farm cottage and broken-down machinery.

*"The sky's pink glow enabled me to capture a certain
image and the result is a subtle and unusual view
of a typically Australian outback scene."*

AIPP

Australian Institute of
Professional Photography

Awards

2000 AIPP   National Professional
Photography Awards
Landscape - Four Silver

2000 AIPP   Canon Queensland Professional
Photography Awards
Highest Scoring Colour Print
Landscape - One Gold & Four Silver

1999 AIPP   Australian Institute of Professional
Photography Awards
Landscape - Silver with distinction
& One Silver

1999 AIPP   Canon Queensland Professional
Photography Awards
One Silver

1999 Fuji ACMP   Australian Photographers
Collection Six
Honour of Recognition

Peter Lik, Australia's award-winning panoramic photographer now proudly presents his own galleries. His highly successful publishing company, *Peter Lik's Wilderness Press*, was born in Cairns just three years ago, providing the marketplace with stylish books and postcards featuring Peter's distinctive imagery.

Signed limited edition prints of Peter's spectacular images are available at the galleries.

Peter Lik's Wilderness Press mirrors the same enthusiasm and innovative approach to photography as its founder and will continue to expand as a public showcase of Peter's outstanding images.

Galleries located at:

Cairns	4 Shields Street.	Tel: **(07) 4031 8177**
Port Douglas	19 Macrossan St.	Tel: **(07) 4099 6050**
Sydney	QVB, 455 George St.	Tel: **(02) 9269 0182**
San Francisco USA	Pier 39, 94119	
Monterey USA	Cannery Row, 93940	

"I exclusively use Fuji Professional film and cameras to capture the true colours of Australia.

I find Fuji velvia film delivers vivid colour saturation and superb clarity under whatever light conditions there are.

For the high standards of this book, there was no other choice."

Front Cover - **The Twelve Apostles**, *Victoria*
Back Cover - **Lone Shack**, *Outback Queensland*

ISBN 9781876585037

© Wilderness Press 1999 Reprinted 2000, 2001

® Panoscapes is a registered trademark of
Peter Lik's Wilderness Press Pty Ltd

Published by Wilderness Press, an imprint of
Peter Lik's Wilderness Press Pty Ltd

Text by Robert Reid
Designed by Peter Lik & Stephen Borzi

PO Box 2529 Cairns Queensland 4870 Australia

Email **info@peterlik.com.au**

Telephone **(07) 4053 9000** Fax (07) 4032 1277

WEBSITE **www.peterlik.com**

PeterLik**Publishing**

PETER LIK IMAGES ARE EXCLUSIVELY REPRESENTED BY:

PETER**LIK**IMAGE**LIBRARY**

Telephone 1800 135 617   www.peterlikimages.com

This book is dedicated to my Mum & Dad.

Hopeton Falls, Otway Ranges, Victoria

1999 AIPP Australian Professional Photography Awards. Silver with Distinction awarded – Landscape Category.